Dear Parent,

In <u>Why Is the Sky Blue?</u> your child will learn the meaning of the words atmosphere and molecule. Crow uses brightly colored crayons and a big chart to show Christopher and his friends why the sky is blue and why it is sometimes pink and sometimes gray. Pack a lunch and join Christopher for a picnic under the sunny blue sky.

Sincerely,

Rita D. Gould

Managing Editor

FAMILY FUN

- Make a Sky Book with your child. Help your child cut from magazines pictures of people doing everyday activities when the sky is blue, cloudy, or rainy. Then paste the pictures onto pieces of cardboard. Help your child write a few lines about each picture on each piece of cardboard. Tie the cardboard pieces together with a colorful ribbon and read the book with your child.

READ MORE ABOUT IT

- *What Is a Rainbow?*
- *What Is a Cloud?*
- *Why Does It Rain?*

D1738808

This book is a presentation of Weekly Reader
Books. Weekly Reader Books offers book
clubs for children from preschool through high
school. For further information write to:
WEEKLY READER BOOKS, 4343 Equity Drive,
Columbus, Ohio 43228

This edition is published by arrangement
with Checkerboard Press.

Weekly Reader is a federally registered trademark
of Field Publications.

WEEKLY READER BOOKS presents

Why Is the Sky Blue?

A **Just Ask**™ Book

Hi, my name is
Christopher

by Chris Arvetis
and Carole Palmer

illustrated by
James Buckley

FIELD PUBLICATIONS
MIDDLETOWN, CT.

But look at the sky.
See how blue it is.
It probably won't
rain today.

I'll try to answer, but that is a hard question.

First of all, you have to learn about the sky.

Sky is a word we use to name all of the air above us.

It is the earth's ATMOSPHERE.

That's a big word!

Say it with me.

The earth's atmosphere is made up of many little parts called MOLECULES. That's another gigantic word— say MOL-E-CULES!

When the sun rises and sets, a lot of blue light is lost. We see the red or pink colors. Those are the colors we see in the sky at sunrise and sunset.

On a very cloudy or rainy day, some of the light is stopped by all the clouds.

We see only the gray or milky white sky— no pretty colors.